To

_____

From

_____

Date

_____

Message

_____

_____

_____

_____

BOOK of PRAYERS

The Power of
PRAYING®
THROUGH
Fear

STORMIE
OMARTIAN

HARVEST HOUSE PUBLISHERS
EUGENE, OREGON

Cover by Bryce Williamson

Cover Image © axllll /iStock

Back cover author photo © Michael Gomez Photography

**THE POWER OF PRAYING® THROUGH FEAR
BOOK OF PRAYERS**
Copyright © 2017 by Stormie Omartian
Published by Harvest House Publishers
Eugene, Oregon 97408
www.harvesthousepublishers.com

ISBN 978-0-7369-6701-3 (pbk.)
ISBN 978-0-7369-6702-0 (eBook)

Printed in the United States of America

18 19 20 21 22 23 24 25 / BP-JC / 10 9 8 7 6 5 4 3 2 1

Introduction

We all need to pray whenever we find ourselves fearful about anything. But sometimes fear can come suddenly and be so overwhelming that we don't know the most powerful way to pray at the time. That's why I have written this little *Book of Prayers*, compiled mostly from my book *The Power of Praying Through Fear*. Also included are prayers I have specifically written for this small book that were inspired by the topics in the big book. I want this *Book of Prayers* to give you a quick and convenient tool to help you combat fear in a big way.

I know from personal experience how upsetting and tormenting fear can be, and God doesn't want us to live that way. He wants us to draw close to Him so we can understand how much He loves us. He wants us to trust Him to lead us to a place of peace, both within ourselves and also in our physical life. We must have that in order to live the life of purpose He has for us.

Keep this book close at hand so you can pray these powerful prayers based on God's Word whenever you need them to help you find the guidance, comfort, and peace He has for you.

Stormie Omartian

There is no fear in love;
but perfect love casts out fear,
because fear involves torment.
But he who fears has not been
made perfect in love.

1 JOHN 4:18

What Can Fear Do to Us?

Lord, I ask You to reveal any fear I have that is affecting my life negatively so I can be free of it. The only fear I accept is that which You allow to wake me up to what You want me to understand. If I have given a place in my heart to fear, I confess it to You as sin because it reveals my lack of faith in You and Your Word to protect me. Forgive me and help me to stand strong against fear so I can be set completely free. Thank You that You have given me Your unconditional and perfect love that casts out all fear (1 John 4:18).

In Jesus' name I pray.

The LORD is my light and my salvation;
whom shall I fear?
The LORD is the strength of my life;
of whom shall I be afraid?

PSALM 27:1

Prayer Notes

_____
_____
_____
_____
_____
_____
_____
_____
_____
_____
_____
_____
_____

What Can Fear Do to Us?

Lord, Thank You that You have given me access to Your power through Your Holy Spirit, which enables me to live the life You have for me. Teach me to claim the clear and sound mind You have given me so I can stand strong against any error of thinking or instability in my mind.

Help me to never give place to irrational fear or allow it to occupy my mind or my life in any way. Show me where fear in me has brought about illness or infirmity of any kind so I can be healed. Keep my heart strong so that it never fails because of fear. Thank You that You are far greater than anything I fear.

In Jesus' name I pray.

Why are you cast down, O my soul?
And why are you disquieted within me?
Hope in God, for I shall yet praise Him
for the help of His countenance.

Psalm 42:5

Prayer Notes

_____

_____

_____

_____

_____

_____

_____

_____

_____

_____

_____

What Can Fear Do to Us?

Lord, I pray You will show me if I have allowed the negative results of fear to overtake my life and make me mentally, emotionally, or physically weakened. I don't want to lose my joy, energy, strength, and hope. I don't want fear to incapacitate me with anxiety and the inability to think clearly. I want *You* to control my life and not my own fear. Thank You that a spirit of fear is never from You. Thank You that, instead, You have given me Your love, Your power, and nothing less than the sound mind You have for me. I invite Your transforming love and power to work in and through me to help me rise above all fear every day.

In Jesus' name I pray.

Say to those who are fearful-hearted,
"Be strong, do not fear!
Behold, your God will come with vengeance,
with the recompense of God;
He will come and save you."

ISAIAH 35:4

Prayer Notes

What Can Fear Do to Us?

Lord, I pray You will set me free from any "What if?" thoughts that come to my mind. They incapacitate me, make my life feel out of control, and rob me of the peace You have for me. Teach me how to take every thought captive and bring my concerns before You so that they will not have power to cause doubt in me. I ask You to be in control of my life so I am free of the stranglehold of fear. I don't want the fear in me to ever come close to being greater than my faith in You and in Your ability to do a miracle in my life. Give me the strength and power I need to live unafraid because I live for You.

In Jesus' name I pray.

Wait on the LORD; be of good courage,
and He shall strengthen your heart;
wait, I say, on the LORD!

PSALM 27:14

Prayer Notes

_____

_____

_____

_____

_____

_____

_____

_____

_____

_____

_____

What Can Fear Do to Us?

Lord, thank You that the truth of Your Word sets me free. In this world where bad news travels fast, I pray my knowledge of Your Word is far greater than my awareness of the frightening things happening around me. Your Word speaks of people's hearts failing because of fear (Luke 21:26). I pray that will never happen to me. I pray that my health and strength will never be weakened because of fear. Help me to walk through my life on the solid foundation of Your Word. Grow my faith in Your Word to be far greater than my fear. Help me to read and understand Your Word so I can quickly speak it out loud in the face of any fear.

In Jesus' name I pray.

If you abide in My word,
you are My disciples indeed.
And you shall know the truth,
and the truth shall make you free.

JOHN 8:31-32

Prayer Notes

_____
_____
_____
_____
_____
_____
_____
_____
_____
_____
_____

What Can Fear Do to Us?

Lord, help me to see where fear is affecting my life in a negative way, such as my sleep, health, work, relationships, decisions, and ability to do what I need to do. Show me how to get free of fear so I can move into all You have for me. Help me to remember that I am Your child, and a life of fear is not what You have for me. I reject anything in my past that has made me fearful now. Help me to focus entirely on You and not on the source of my fear. Keep me from ever becoming so rigid that I can't let go of past fears and learn to live in the freedom and wholeness You have for me.

In Jesus' name I pray.

*The Spirit Himself bears witness with our spirit
that we are children of God,
and if children, then heirs—
heirs of God and joint heirs with Christ,
if indeed we suffer with Him,
that we may also be glorified together.*

ROMANS 8:16-17

Prayer Notes

_____

_____

_____

_____

_____

_____

_____

_____

_____

_____

_____

_____

What Do We Fear Most?

Lord, where I have allowed dark memories from my past to affect my life in a negative way, I pray You would shine Your light on them now so I can be free of them. Lift me out of that and move me forward into the new life You have for me. Enable me to stand strong in You and never give in to fear or discouragement. Teach me how to believe and speak Your Word whenever fear threatens to weaken me and keep me from rising above it. Teach me to face any dark memories with Your presence walking me through them. Enable me not to fear the dark places in me, especially when I think I have finally gotten rid of them and then some surface again. Keep me focused on You.

In Jesus' name I pray.

I sought the LORD, and He heard me,
and delivered me from all my fears.

PSALM 34:4

Prayer Notes

_____

_____

_____

_____

_____

_____

_____

_____

_____

_____

What Do We Fear Most?

Lord, open my spiritual eyes, ears, and heart to hear Your Spirit speaking to me. Show me any place in my mind where a specific fear has taken hold that will keep me from the liberty You have for me. I ask that You will be fully in control of my life so that I can be a slave to Your righteousness and not a slave to fear. Teach me to live in and be motivated by Your perfect love, which casts out tormenting fear (1 John 4:18). Thank You, Lord, that You are able to deliver me from all my fears (Psalm 34:4). I ask You to do that now.

In Jesus' name I pray.

There is no fear in love;
but perfect love casts out fear,
because fear involves torment.
But he who fears has not been made
perfect in love.

1 John 4:18

Prayer Notes

What Do We Fear Most?

Lord, if I am ever talking to people—whether just a few or many—and become anxious or afraid, I pray You will help me remember who I am in You. I pray this knowledge will take away all my fear and give me Your strength, power, and clarity of mind. Give me Your love for each person I talk to, and help me to see them through *Your* eyes. Open their spiritual eyes, ears, and heart to hear Your Spirit speaking to them.

Teach me to pray about each fear I have with regard to speaking in front of, or even just being with, a group of people. Help me to stop thinking about myself and think about the people I am talking to and how much they need to sense Your love.

In Jesus' name I pray.

*Out of much affliction and
anguish of heart I wrote to you,
with many tears, not that you should be grieved,
but that you might know the love
which I have so abundantly for you.*

2 Corinthians 2:4

Prayer Notes

_____

_____

_____

_____

_____

_____

_____

_____

_____

_____

_____

What Do We Fear Most?

Lord, I am afraid as I see the evil around me increasing and dangerous leaders threatening to destroy many people. I know only You can lead those of us who love You into the safety and peace we all want and need. Your Word says, "Why should I fear in the days of evil, when the iniquity at my heels surrounds me?" (Psalm 49:5). It is because You have power far greater than any power on this earth that resists You and Your laws. I pray no weapon formed against us will prosper. Raise up an army of Your prayer warriors who know the power of prayer in Jesus' name to bring down strongholds and all who exalt themselves against You and Your people.

In Jesus' name I pray.

The LORD is my helper; I will not fear.
What can man do to me?

HEBREWS 13:6

Prayer Notes

_____

_____

_____

_____

_____

_____

_____

_____

_____

_____

What Do We Fear Most?

Lord, sometimes I'm afraid of being rejected by people. But Your Word says, "The fear of man brings a snare, but whoever trusts in the LORD shall be safe" (Proverbs 29:25). Help me to trust in You so completely that I do not fall into the trap of fearing rejection. Take away all fear so that I am not weakened or restricted by it and, because of that, fail to do what You have called me to do. Thank You, Jesus, that You suffered the worst rejection so that we who love You can be forever accepted by You and dwell with You in eternity. Help me to live in Your love, knowing I am never rejected by You.

In Your name I pray.

In You, O LORD, I put my trust;
let me never be ashamed;
deliver me in Your righteousness.

PSALM 31:1

Prayer Notes

What Do We Fear Most?

Lord, I'm afraid of unending pain and suffering. I've experienced enough of that in my life to know I don't want to go through it again. I also fear a lack of provision, but I know from Your Word that You will supply all my needs—whether they are spiritual, physical, or material. Help me to trust that Your goodness toward me will never fail and that Your love for me is greater than anything I fear. I confess that anytime I question Your ability to supply all that I need, it's a sign of doubt. And doubt is sin because whatever is not showing strong faith in You is sin. Free me from doubt and increase my faith in You and Your Word.

In Jesus' name I pray.

My God shall supply all your need
according to His riches in glory by Christ Jesus.

PHILIPPIANS 4:19

Prayer Notes

_____

_____

_____

_____

_____

_____

_____

_____

_____

_____

_____

What Does the Bible
Say About Fear?

Lord, thank You for Your grace, which has saved me in every way I can be saved. Thank You that in Your mercy You have given me Your love to strengthen and heal me and take away my fear. Thank You for Your Word that reminds me You are *with* me and *for* me at all times. Therefore, I do not need to live in fear about who is against me. With You on my side, who can have victory over me?

Enable me to grow with unshakable faith in You and to live my life according to the leading of Your Holy Spirit. Engrave Your Word on my heart so I never forget it.

In Jesus' name I pray.

God is our refuge and strength,
a very present help in trouble.

PSALM 46:1

Prayer Notes

_____
_____
_____
_____
_____
_____
_____
_____
_____
_____
_____
_____

What Does the Bible Say About Fear?

Lord, help me to keep Your truth in my mind at all times so it becomes part of me. Thank You that out of my heart "flow rivers of living water" that come from Your Holy Spirit in me (John 7:38). Help me to never stop that flow by my unbelief. I thank You for Your power to free me from the grip of fear and anxiety. Protect me from the things I fear and from all dangers lurking about that I am not even aware of yet. Teach me to never forget that You are always with me. Help me to do all I need to do. Thank You that You love me and I am valuable to You.

In Jesus' name I pray.

The LORD is good,
a stronghold in the day of trouble;
and He knows those who trust in Him.

NAHUM 1:7

Prayer Notes

_____

_____

_____

_____

_____

_____

_____

_____

_____

_____

_____

What Does the Bible Say About Fear?

Lord, set me free from all fear and anxiety. Take away any feelings I have of being overwhelmed by them. I want to say as David did—when he prayed day and night, trusting You heard his prayers—You have "redeemed my soul in peace from the battle that was against me" (Psalm 55:18). Help me to truly "be anxious for nothing," pray about everything, and be thankful to You (Philippians 4:6). Your Word promises that when I do that, I will have peace that is beyond what I can imagine, and it will guard my heart (verse 7). Help me to live every day with a grateful heart so I don't have to needlessly and hopelessly suffer with fear and anxiety.

In Jesus' name I pray.

This poor man cried out,
and the LORD heard him,
and saved him out of all his troubles.

PSALM 34:6

Prayer Notes

_____

_____

_____

_____

_____

_____

_____

_____

_____

_____

_____

What Does the Bible
Say About Fear?

Lord, I am grateful that You can do what I fear I cannot do on my own. I don't know how to protect myself and my loved ones from danger, but You do. Thank You for Your grace that allows Your Holy Spirit to work powerfully in my life when I have done nothing to deserve it. Thank You that I don't have to achieve great things on my own, but by Your power and strength working through me, I can do what You call me to do. I trust Your Word that says You will never leave me nor forsake me (Hebrews 13:5). When I'm afraid, help me to seek Your presence and walk closely with You, trusting You will calm my heart.

In Jesus' name I pray.

Fear not, for I am with you;
be not dismayed, for I am your God.
I will strengthen you, yes, I will help you,
I will uphold you with My righteous right hand.

Isaiah 41:10

Prayer Notes

_____

_____

_____

_____

_____

_____

_____

_____

_____

_____

What Does the Bible
Say About Fear?

Lord, help me to have strong faith in You and Your Word. I want my faith to be so strong that it will not fail me in times of fear and weakness. Jesus, You prayed for Your disciples that their faith "should not fail" (Luke 22:32). I, too, pray that my faith will not fail in frightening times in my life. Help me to "walk by faith, not by sight" (2 Corinthians 5:7). Enable me to focus on Your power instead of on what frightens me, knowing that nothing is impossible for You. You have said, "All things are possible to him who believes" (Mark 9:23). I choose to believe that promise with all my heart. Help me to not have doubt when fear threatens to overwhelm me.

In Your name I pray.

Faith is the substance of things hoped for,
the evidence of things not seen.

Hebrews 11:1

Prayer Notes

What Does the Bible Say About Fear?

Lord, Your Word assures me that You know those who are Yours (2 Timothy 2:19). Thank You that You will never abandon me, for You are always with me. Perfect Your love in me so that I can sense Your comforting presence with me. Thank You that I will not receive "the spirit of bondage again to fear" because I am Yours (Romans 8:15). Your Word says not to "fear when heat comes," and not to "be anxious in the year of drought" (Jeremiah 17:8). Help me to remember that when the heat is on in my life, I won't wither under the pressure. And when I lack provision, I don't have to fear because You will supply my needs.

In Jesus' name I pray.

Fear not, for I have redeemed you;
I have called you by your name; you are Mine.

ISAIAH 43:1

Prayer Notes

_____

_____

_____

_____

_____

_____

_____

_____

_____

_____

_____

What Is the Fear God Allows Us to Experience?

Lord, help me to clearly discern the promptings of Your Spirit to my heart and mind so that I never foolishly ignore them. Teach me to pray whenever I have fear or a sense of danger or intuition about persons or situations that are not good. Keep me and my family and friends away from dangerous places and always aware of the possible plans of evil people. Give us discernment and warnings when we are not where we are supposed to be.

Help me to reverence You with all my heart and not depend on my own understanding. Help me to know when the fear I have is what You have allowed in my life in order to get my attention and help me hear Your instructions.

In Jesus' name I pray.

You did not choose Me,
but I chose you and appointed you
that you should go and bear fruit,
and that your fruit should remain,
that whatever you ask the Father in My name
He may give you.

JOHN 15:16

Prayer Notes

What Is the Fear God Allows Us to Experience?

Lord, keep me from assuming anything by neglecting to take everything to You. I don't ever want to think I know everything about a person, place, or situation. I want to hear the truth from You.

Help me to choose every day to walk with the leading of Your Holy Spirit and not be led by my flesh. Produce in me the fruit of Your Spirit. Fill me with Your love, peace, and joy so that I will be more like You. Make me patient, kind, and good to others. Cause me to be faithful and gentle and always exhibiting great self-control. Teach me to pray unceasingly about everything so I will always know when You are allowing me to experience fear for my own good.

In Jesus' name I pray.

*The fruit of the Spirit is love, joy, peace,
longsuffering, kindness, goodness, faithfulness,
gentleness, self-control.*

GALATIANS 5:22-23

Prayer Notes

_____

_____

_____

_____

_____

_____

_____

_____

_____

_____

_____

_____

What Is the Fear God Allows Us to Experience?

Lord, Your Word says, "If you do evil, be afraid" (Romans 13:4). If there is something I am doing that is not right in Your sight, help me to hear Your guidance concerning it. Thank You for the fear You allow in my life that brings me closer to You. Give me discernment so I can always hear Your instruction to my heart. Deliver me from evil so that I am not led astray. Help me to bear good fruit in my life so that You are glorified in all I do. Teach me to be a disciple of Yours so that I will fulfill Your purpose for my life. Help me to understand when the fear I have is something You have allowed to keep me dependent on You.

In Jesus' name I pray.

By this My Father is glorified,
that you bear much fruit;
so you will be My disciples.

John 15:8

Prayer Notes

_____

_____

_____

_____

_____

_____

_____

_____

_____

_____

_____

_____

What Is the Fear God Allows Us to Experience?

Lord, just as David prayed that You would keep him from "secret faults" and "presumptuous sins," I pray that for me as well (Psalm 19:12-13). Help me to never assume anything without talking to You about it first and reading Your Word every day to be reminded of the truth about You and Your ways. Enable me to see every warning of danger within Your Word that I must never forget. I don't want to ever get to the point where I think I always know Your will for me in every situation. Teach me to seek You in order to know Your will in my life each day. Keep me sensitive to what You are telling me regarding any fear I feel.

In Jesus' name I pray.

The fear of the LORD is clean, enduring forever;
the judgments of the LORD are true and
righteous altogether...
Moreover by them Your servant is warned,
and in keeping them there is great reward.

PSALM 19:9,11

Prayer Notes

_____

_____

_____

_____

_____

_____

_____

_____

_____

_____

_____

_____

What Is the Fear God Allows Us to Experience?

Lord, help me to always hear Your voice to my heart leading me to the right place at the right time. Don't let me ignore the instructions or warnings You give me, for Your Word says, "He who is of God hears God's words" (John 8:47).

Teach me to examine every fear I have to see if You are allowing it in order to keep me close to You. Teach me to discern the prompting of Your Spirit. I want to always be led by You in the way You want me to go. Help me to never push aside an uneasy feeling about a person or situation. Be in charge of my life, and always show me what I should do or *not* do.

In Jesus' name I pray.

"For the oppression of the poor,
for the sighing of the needy,
now I will arise," says the LORD;
"I will set him in the safety for which he yearns."

PSALM 12:5

Prayer Notes

What Is the Fear God Allows Us to Experience?

Lord, I ask You to help me be wise about the people I spend time with. Give me the discernment I need in order to know if it's Your will that I give them close access to my life or the lives of my children. I need to hear Your voice to my heart guiding me in all things. Don't let me ignore Your leading with regard to possible dangers in my life or in the lives of my loved ones. I want to be able to love others the way You want me to and yet be fully aware when someone is not who they appear to be. I need Your power working in me so I can do what You want me to do.

In Jesus' name I pray.

Please, obey the voice of the LORD
which I speak to you.
So it shall be well with you,
and your soul shall live.

JEREMIAH 38:20

Prayer Notes

What Is the Fear God
Wants Us to Have?

Lord, I want to be the "companion of all who fear You, and of those who keep Your precepts" (Psalm 119:63). "Teach me Your way, O LORD; I will walk in Your truth; unite my heart to fear Your name" (Psalm 86:11). Enable me to be filled with the knowledge of Your will. Give me the wisdom, discernment, and spiritual understanding to walk in ways that are pleasing to You.

Teach me to treasure Your commands and laws in my heart at all times. Help me to acknowledge You in everything I do so You can direct my paths. Enable me to live in Your presence, because every time I sense Your presence, it takes away all my fear.

In Jesus' name I pray.

Come, you children, listen to me;
I will teach you the fear of the LORD.

PSALM 34:11

Prayer Notes

What Is the Fear God Wants Us to Have?

Lord, help me to be a true God-fearing person. Give me godly wisdom so that I don't fall for the wisdom of this world. Gift me with the knowledge and understanding I need in order to live according to Your plan and purpose. Keep me from ever being wise in my own eyes, but rather help me to fear You and stay away from evil.

Thank You that You give "strength and power" to Your people (Psalm 68:35). Thank You that "You have given me the heritage of those who fear Your name" (Psalm 61:5). My reverence and love for You is true because Your presence in my life is my greatest treasure.

In Jesus' name I pray.

Oh, fear the LORD, you His saints!
There is no want to those who fear Him.
The young lions lack and suffer hunger;
but those who seek the LORD
shall not lack any good thing.

PSALM 34:9-10

Prayer Notes

_____

_____

_____

_____

_____

_____

_____

_____

_____

_____

_____

What Is the Fear God Wants Us to Have?

Lord, I know the only fear You want us to have is fear or reverence of You—fear of what life would be like without You. My heart is full of love, awe, and respect for You, and I thank You for the rewards that come to those who fear You. Thank You for the blessing of answered prayer, guidance, discernment, protection, provision, and the promise of a good and full life. My desire is to walk with You and reverence You in every way that is pleasing to You. Help me to do that. I want to enjoy the love and peace You give to those who fear You, because that takes away the fear You don't want us to have.

In Jesus' name I pray.

He will fulfill the desire of those who fear Him;
He also will hear their cry and save them.

PSALM 145:19

Prayer Notes

What Is the Fear God Wants Us to Have?

Lord, thank You for Your Word that says You watch over those who fear You and who hope in Your mercy (Psalm 33:18). Thank You that Your angels surround me and deliver me because I reverence and serve You. Thank You that those of us who fear You will always find life working out better for us. Because You love us, we are helped and protected, and Your mercy is upon us.

Help me to bless others with the blessings You pour out on me. Enable me to not cower or withdraw from life in fear, but rather to be strong in You so I am a strength to others. Enable me to impart to others the knowledge You have imparted to me.

In Jesus' name I pray.

The angel of the LORD encamps all around
those who fear Him, and delivers them.

PSALM 34:7

Prayer Notes

What Is the Fear God Wants Us to Have?

Lord, Your Word says my fear and reverence of You "is a fountain of life" that will turn me away "from the snares of death" (Proverbs 14:27). Enable me to remember at all times that my faith in and reverence of You give me life. Help me to "keep sound wisdom and discretion" so they will be life to my soul, for then I "will walk safely," and when I lie down I can sleep and "not be afraid" (Proverbs 3:21-24).

I pray You will give me the wisdom and understanding I need at all times, for then I will always reverence You and know the right thing to do. I pray the wisdom and knowledge You give me will strengthen me even in shaky times and uncertain situations.

In Jesus' name I pray.

Do not be wise in your own eyes;
fear the LORD and depart from evil.

PROVERBS 3:7

Prayer Notes

_____

_____

_____

_____

_____

_____

_____

_____

_____

_____

_____

What Is the Fear God Wants Us to Have?

Lord, Your Word makes a great distinction between the wisdom of the world, which comes to nothing, and Your wisdom, which leads to life. Help me to never get confused about that. Give me a heart and mind that can see and discern between what is from You and what is not. Even as I read or hear the news, help me to know what is really true. Keep me from being deceived by what is advanced by ungodly people for their own benefit. Where people try to incite fear in order to gain power over others, enable me to see Your truth through and above it all. Reveal to me everything I need in order to be completely free of fear.

In Jesus' name I pray.

It is already an utter failure for you
that you go to law against one another.
Why do you not rather accept wrong?
Why do you not rather let yourselves be cheated?

1 CORINTHIANS 6:7

Prayer Notes

_____

_____

_____

_____

_____

_____

_____

_____

_____

_____

_____

What Must We Think, Say, and Pray When We Are Afraid?

Lord, help me to remember everything I need to recall from Your Word, especially whenever I am afraid. Enable me to speak Your Word boldly in the face of the things that frighten me. Even if there is no one else around, I will declare what I believe because Your Word gives me strength and peace and builds my faith. Thank You that You have "come as a light into the world," so that whoever believes in You "should not abide in darkness" (John 12:46). I don't have to live in the darkness of fear because I now live in the warmth and protection of Your healing and restoring light. Thank You that You have "overcome the world" (John 16:33).

In Jesus' name I pray.

In the world you will have tribulation;
but be of good cheer,
I have overcome the world.

JOHN 16:33

Prayer Notes

_____

_____

_____

_____

_____

_____

_____

_____

_____

_____

_____

What Must We Think, Say, and Pray When We Are Afraid?

Lord, help me to always watch what I say, for I know that "out of the abundance of the heart the mouth speaks" (Matthew 12:34). Fill my heart with Your love and truth. Enable me to declare Your truth out loud and share it with others. Teach me to "pray without ceasing" (1 Thessalonians 5:17).

Thank You that I don't have to "be afraid of the terror by night, nor of the arrow that flies by day" (Psalm 91:5). Thank You that "You have also given me the shield of Your salvation; Your right hand has held me up, Your gentleness has made me great" (Psalm 18:35). "Whenever I am afraid, I will trust in You" (Psalm 56:3).

In Jesus' name I pray.

*Be anxious for nothing, but in everything
by prayer and supplication, with thanksgiving,
let your requests be made known to God;
and the peace of God, which surpasses
all understanding, will guard your hearts and
minds through Christ Jesus.*

PHILIPPIANS 4:6-7

Prayer Notes

What Must We Think, Say, and Pray When We Are Afraid?

Lord, You are "my helper," so I will not be afraid of what people can do to me (Hebrews 13:6). Thank You that You are with me, and I don't have to live in fear. Thank You that You are always on my side, so evil cannot succeed against me. You are my place of safety and refuge in times of trouble. You are my comfort and strength. You are more powerful than anything I fear. Help me to be confident in You and in Your power, knowing no one is greater than You.

Enable me to remember all these things when I am weakened by sudden fear. Help me to speak Your Word out loud in the face of fear. Teach me to pray in power.

In Jesus' name I pray.

The LORD is on my side; I will not fear.
What can man do to me?

PSALM 118:6

Prayer Notes

What Must We Think, Say, and Pray When We Are Afraid?

Lord, You are my strength. No one is more powerful than You. Because of You I don't have to be afraid "of sudden terror, nor of trouble from the wicked when it comes" (Proverbs 3:25). Keep me out of harm's way, and teach me to pray about everything. Your Word says that no weapon formed against me will be successful, and all the words of evil that are spoken against me will not destroy me (Isaiah 54:17). Thank You that You will protect me from the words and weapons of evil people.

Your Word says, "He shall give His angels charge over you, to keep you in all your ways" (Psalm 91:11). Thank You for surrounding me with Your angels to keep me safe in every way.

In Jesus' name I pray.

*"No weapon formed against you shall prosper,
and every tongue which rises against you
in judgment You shall condemn.
This is the heritage of the servants of the LORD,
and their righteousness is from Me," says the LORD.*

ISAIAH 54:17

Prayer Notes

What Must We Think, Say, and Pray When We Are Afraid?

Lord, I come to You with a grateful heart for Your goodness and mercy poured out on me. With You on my side, who can succeed against me? Thank You that "I can do all things through Christ who strengthens me" (Philippians 4:13). Strengthen me to do what I cannot do without You. Help me rise above my fear so that it does not control my life. Thank You that You love me with unfailing and unconditional love. Fill me to overflowing with Your love so that I am never tormented by fear. Thank You that You have given me Your Holy Spirit to be my Helper and Comforter. I know that with Your great power working in me, I need never be overpowered by fear.

In Jesus' name I pray.

What then shall we say to these things?
If God is for us, who can be against us?

ROMANS 8:31

Prayer Notes

_____

_____

_____

_____

_____

_____

_____

_____

_____

_____

_____

_____

_____

What Must We Think, Say, and Pray When We Are Afraid?

Lord, thank You that You can do beyond what I even ask for or think of because of the power of Your Spirit in me. Thank You that whenever I need a greater sense of Your love, power, and presence in my life, I can come to You, and out of my heart "will flow rivers of living water" (John 7:38). Flow through me now and wash away all my fear. Fill me with Your love, peace, and joy, and bring a fresh flow of healing to my mind, heart, and body. Jesus, You said that if I "ask anything" in Your name, You "will do it" (John 14:14). Thank You for that promise. I pray You will free me from any grip of fear and give me Your peace.

In Your name I pray.

Peace I leave with you,
My peace I give to you;
not as the world gives do I give to you.
Let not your heart be troubled,
neither let it be afraid.

JOHN 14:27

Prayer Notes

What Should We Do When We Feel Fearful?

Lord, help me to do the things I need to do in my life so that whenever I feel afraid, I will have a strong foundation in You already established. I thank You for who You are and all You have done for me. Help me to keep my mind focused on good things and not negative and frightening things.

Help me to always walk in Your ways and keep Your laws and commandments. Keep me from doing anything that compromises my walk with You. "Cause me to hear Your lovingkindness in the morning, for in You do I trust; cause me to know the way in which I should walk, for I lift up my soul to You" (Psalm 143:8).

In Jesus' name I pray.

Put off, concerning your former conduct,
the old man which grows corrupt
according to the deceitful lusts,
and be renewed in the spirit of your mind,
and...put on the new man which was
created according to God,
in true righteousness and holiness.

EPHESIANS 4:22-24

Prayer Notes

What Should We Do
When We Feel Fearful?

Lord, enable me to do the right things and stop doing the things that are not good for my life. Help me to forgive when I need to forgive and not hold on to thoughts of vengeance. Help me to get rid of all temptation to do otherwise. Show me anything I need to stop doing because it is not Your best for my life. Teach me to share the good things You have done for me with others who need to hear it. Enable me to give to You and to others in the way You want me to. Help me to do what I need to do to keep fear away from my life.

In Jesus' name I pray.

Whatever you do in word or deed,
do all in the name of the Lord Jesus,
giving thanks to God the Father through Him.

COLOSSIANS 3:17

Prayer Notes

_____
_____
_____
_____
_____
_____
_____
_____
_____
_____
_____

What Should We Do
When We Feel Fearful?

Lord, I pray You would enable me to bring every thought captive. Help me to pull down any stronghold of fear and anxiety that has been erected in my mind. Enable me to stand strong in refusing to allow my own negative thoughts to weaken me with fear. I commit everything I do to You so I can walk closely with You and serve You. Your Word says to "commit your works to the LORD, and your thoughts will be established" (Proverbs 16:3). I commit everything I do to You. Establish my thoughts in clarity and calmness every day so I don't live in fear that some terrible thing will creep into my life and take away my peace.

In Jesus' name I pray.

*The weapons of our warfare are not carnal
but mighty in God for pulling down strongholds,
casting down arguments and every high thing
that exalts itself against the knowledge of God,
bringing every thought into captivity
to the obedience of Christ.*

2 Corinthians 10:4-5

Prayer Notes

What Should We Do
When We Feel Fearful?

Lord, I worship You for who You are and all You have done for me. You are the almighty God of the universe, Creator of all things, who has rescued me from hopelessness, futility, and fear. I praise You in all situations—whether good or bad—because You are always good and Your love and mercy extended to me never ceases. Your Word says You are enthroned in our praises (Psalm 22:3). Thank You that Your presence is with me in greater measure every time I worship You. In Your presence my life is changed, and the doors to my personal prison are opened. Thank You in advance for setting me free from all fear and the conditions that have caused it.

In Jesus' name I pray.

I will bless the LORD at all times;
His praise shall continually be in my mouth.
My soul shall make its boast in the LORD;
the humble shall hear of it and be glad.
Oh, magnify the LORD with me,
and let us exalt His name together.
I sought the LORD, and He heard me,
and delivered me from all my fears.

PSALM 34:1-4

Prayer Notes

What Should We Do
When We Feel Fearful?

Lord, help me to take control of my mind by deliberately thinking about the truth of Your Word and all that is right and just. Teach me to dwell on things that are lovely and not ugly, pure and not corrupt. Enable me to search for the good news and not fixate on everything that is bad. I want to think about all that is praiseworthy, and all that is morally good and desirable in Your eyes. Help me to focus on You and Your Word every day and throughout all my days. Help me to see anything I am doing, thinking, saying, or entertaining in my mind or heart that is not part of Your perfect will for my life.

In Jesus' name I pray.

Whatever things are true, whatever things are noble,
whatever things are just, whatever things are pure,
whatever things are lovely,
whatever things are of good report,
if there is any virtue and
if there is anything praiseworthy—
meditate on these things.

PHILIPPIANS 4:8

Prayer Notes

What Should We Do
When We Feel Fearful?

Lord Jesus, help me to show my love for You by living Your way. You have said in Your Word, "He who has My commandments and keeps them, it is he who loves Me" (John 14:21). Enable me to be a person after Your own heart who is humble, teachable, and repentant. Keep me from doing anything that will compromise my walk with You. Strengthen me so I can always resist anything that would tempt me away from all You have for me and who You have called me to be. Show me any person, activity, or situation in my life that should not be there, and I will depart from them or that immediately. Open my eyes to see the truth about myself and my situation.

In Your name I pray.

Watch and pray, lest you enter into temptation.
The spirit indeed is willing, but the flesh is weak.

MATTHEW 26:41

Prayer Notes

_____

_____

_____

_____

_____

_____

_____

_____

_____

_____

_____

What Are the Enemy's Fear Tactics?

Thank You, Jesus, that You have made me an heir with You of all that our heavenly Father has for His children. Thank You for the great hope I have in You because You protect me from the enemy when I live Your way and pray according to Your will. Thank You for paying the ultimate price to win the war against Your enemy and mine.

Help me to build my life on the strength of my relationship with You and upon the solid rock of Your Word. Protect me from every lie of the enemy so that I'm never swayed from Your truth. Reveal to me any lies I am believing that cause me to be afraid.

In Your name I pray.

By this I know that You are well pleased with me,
because my enemy does not triumph over me.

PSALM 41:11

Prayer Notes

_____

_____

_____

_____

_____

_____

_____

_____

_____

_____

_____

What Are the Enemy's Fear Tactics?

Lord, help me to depart from evil and never drift away from Your truth. I know that "though an army may encamp against me, my heart shall not fear" because You are with me (Psalm 27:3).

Enable me to always hear the voice of Your Holy Spirit leading me to pray and empowering me to stand strong against the enemy. Show me where my prayer is most needed for myself, my family, and the people and situations You put on my heart. Help me to not think of prayer as merely asking You to fix things, but rather as the way to do battle and take dominion over the works of darkness, as You have said to do.

In Jesus' name I pray.

Blessed is the Lord God of Israel,
for He has visited and redeemed His people...
that we should be saved from our enemies and
from the hand of all who hate us...
to grant us that we, being delivered from the hand of
our enemies, might serve Him without fear,
in holiness and righteousness
before Him all the days of our life.

LUKE 1:68,71,74-75

Prayer Notes

What Are the Enemy's Fear Tactics?

Lord Jesus, thank You for giving me authority to pray in Your name and to know You hear and will answer my prayers according to Your will. Help me to use the authority You have given me in prayer to advance Your kingdom on earth. Teach me how to put on the spiritual armor You have given me so that I and my loved ones and the people I care about are protected and prepared for any plan of the enemy to destroy us. Thank You, Lord, that You "will deliver me from every evil work and preserve me" for Your "heavenly kingdom" (2 Timothy 4:18). Deliver me "from fear of the enemy" (Psalm 64:1). In You, Lord, I have put my trust.

In Your name I pray.

The LORD is my light and my salvation;
whom shall I fear?
The LORD is the strength of my life;
of whom shall I be afraid?...
Though an army may encamp against me,
my heart shall not fear.

PSALM 27:1,3

Prayer Notes

_____

_____

_____

_____

_____

_____

_____

_____

_____

_____

What Are the Enemy's Fear Tactics?

Lord Jesus, thank You that although the enemy comes to steal, kill, and destroy my life, You came to earth so that I may have a more abundant life (John 10:10). Help me to never be deceived by the enemy and allow him to destroy my health, mind, family, marriage, finances, aspirations, or purpose. Teach me to be vigilant in prayer and in obedience to Your ways because "the devil walks about like a roaring lion, seeking whom he may devour" (1 Peter 5:8). Enable me to take back anything the enemy has stolen. Keep me aware of the enemy's tactics so that I never fall into his trap. Thank You for paying the price to break the enemy's power in my life.

In Your name I pray.

*The thief does not come except to steal,
and to kill, and to destroy.
I have come that they may have life,
and that they may have it more abundantly.*

JOHN 10:10

Prayer Notes

_____

_____

_____

_____

_____

_____

_____

_____

_____

_____

What Are the Enemy's Fear Tactics?

Lord Jesus, help me to quickly recognize the lies of the enemy. Fill me with the knowledge of Your truth so I can instantly spot a counterfeit. Thank You that I can know the truth that sets me free and reject the lies of the enemy that can imprison me. Help me to never align myself with the father of lies, but rather align myself with You—the way, the truth, and the life.

Strengthen me to resist the lies of the enemy that would tell me I am a failure and not worthy of Your answers to my prayers. Thank You that Your truth for my life is "there is therefore now no condemnation to those who are in Christ Jesus" (Romans 8:1).

In Your name I pray.

*The Lord is faithful, who will establish you
and guard you from the evil one.*

2 Thessalonians 3:3

Prayer Notes

_____

_____

_____

_____

_____

_____

_____

_____

_____

_____

_____

What Are the Enemy's Fear Tactics?

Lord, help me to keep in mind that Your enemy is my enemy, and he is always in a war against me. I align myself with You and give You my burdens in prayer. Help me to "abstain from every form of evil" (1 Thessalonians 5:22). Keep me from going along with anything the enemy wants to draw me into, which is never of You. I know that "when the enemy comes in like a flood," Your Spirit "will lift up a standard against him" (Isaiah 59:19).

Thank You that You are faithful, and You will establish me and guard me from the evil one (2 Thessalonians 3:3). "Though an army may encamp against me, my heart shall not fear" (Psalm 27:3).

In Jesus' name I pray.

Let love be without hypocrisy.
Abhor what is evil.
Cling to what is good.

ROMANS 12:9

Prayer Notes

What Overcomes the
Fear of Death?

Lord, I pray You will prepare me to be with You someday in heaven. Take away any fear I have about that. I pray I will not die in some horrible, tragic, awful, suffering death. I pray I can die peacefully, surrounded by loving family members and friends. Usher me into Your presence in a way that allows others to see Your glory and goodness. I know that "to be absent from the body" is to be present with You (2 Corinthians 5:8). I look forward to being in Your presence forever. Thank You that because I have received You as my Lord, my name is written in the Lamb's Book of Life.

In Jesus' name I pray.

God will redeem my soul
from the power of the grave,
for He shall receive me.

PSALM 49:15

Prayer Notes

_____

_____

_____

_____

_____

_____

_____

_____

_____

_____

_____

What Overcomes the
Fear of Death?

Lord, help me to live the life You have for me in such a way that I am well prepared to be with You in heaven. I want to hear You say, "Well done, My good and faithful servant." Only You can enable me to do that.

During the moments before my death, I pray I will see a glorious vision of You, Jesus, or the angels You have sent to usher me into Your presence. Use me to show others who are with me that there is nothing to fear in death—and that death is a new and glorious beginning with You and the believers and saints who have gone before us to be with You.

In Jesus' name I pray.

If we live, we live to the Lord;
and if we die, we die to the Lord.
Therefore, whether we live or die,
we are the Lord's.

ROMANS 14:8

Prayer Notes

What Overcomes the
Fear of Death?

Lord, I pray You would help me to understand my final resting place with You. Take away all fear I have about dying so that I don't have to be worried about it. Help me to see in Your Word what heaven is like and to trust that You will raise me "up at the last day" (John 6:44). Because I have chosen to make my final home with You in eternity, I want to be fully prepared for the transition from this life on earth to the next one with You. That's why I ask You to help me walk closely with You. Teach me to settle that transition in my mind and heart, so that my trust in You keeps me from living in fear of death.

In Jesus' name I pray.

If the Spirit of Him who raised Jesus
from the dead dwells in you,
He who raised Christ from the dead will also
give life to your mortal bodies
through His Spirit who dwells in you.

ROMANS 8:11

Prayer Notes

What Overcomes the
Fear of Death?

Lord Jesus, You assure us in Your Word that if we have received You, our names "are written in the Lamb's Book of Life" (Revelation 21:27). Thank You that the moment I received You, my name was written in that book. It gives me great comfort to know I will be with You in eternity. Thank You that You overcame death and hell for me and all who receive You. Keep me from ever stepping outside of Your will for anything. But if I do, lead me to repentance before You so I can be fully restored to You. Your Word says that "he who does the will of God abides forever" (1 John 2:17). Keep me protected in Your will at all times.

In Your name I pray.

I saw the dead, small and great, standing before God,
and books were opened.
And another book was opened,
which is the Book of Life.
And the dead were judged according to their works,
by the things which were written in the books...
And anyone not found written in the Book of Life
was cast into the lake of fire.

REVELATION 20:12,15

Prayer Notes

What Overcomes the
Fear of Death?

Lord Jesus, create in me a clean heart, and renew a right spirit within me. Help me to choose to have a good and positive attitude at all times. You have said in Your Word that "not everyone who says to Me, 'Lord, Lord,' shall enter the kingdom of heaven, but he who does the will of My Father in heaven" (Matthew 7:21). Teach me to come to You in repentance and confession if I ever stray from the path You have for me. I know that when my heart is clean before You, and I have a right and unwavering spirit within me, I will be free of fear—including the fear of death. Keep me in Your perfect will at all times.

In Jesus' name I pray.

Create in me a clean heart, O God,
and renew a steadfast spirit within me.

Psalm 51:10

Prayer Notes

_____

_____

_____

_____

_____

_____

_____

_____

_____

_____

_____

_____

What Overcomes the
Fear of Death?

Lord, thank You that You care about the death of Your people, and my death is precious to You. Thank You that You have prepared a place for each of us, and that includes me. Thank You that my fear of being forgotten cannot happen because Your Spirit in me will lead me home.

I pray as David did, "Though I walk through the valley of the shadow of death, I will fear no evil; for You are with me; Your rod and Your staff, they comfort me" (Psalm 23:4). I know You will be with me and deliver me from any fear of death. Your Word says that "whoever calls on the name of the LORD shall be saved" (Romans 10:13). That is a great comfort to me.

In Jesus' name I pray.

Precious in the sight of the LORD
is the death of His saints.

PSALM 116:15

Prayer Notes

_____

_____

_____

_____

_____

_____

_____

_____

_____

_____

_____

_____

_____

What Can Keep Us from Fearing the Future?

Lord, I thank You that You have given me "a future and a hope" (Jeremiah 29:11). Thank You that because I love You and walk with You and live Your way, I have a good future ahead. Take away all my fears about the future. No matter what in the world I hear, help me to depend only on Your truth and Your love and power in my life. This is the day You have made, and I "will rejoice and be glad in it" (Psalm 118:24).

Thank You that You are "a sun and shield" to me, and You "give grace and glory" and "no good thing" will You withhold "from those who walk uprightly" (Psalm 84:11).

In Jesus' name I pray.

I know the thoughts that I think toward you,
says the LORD,
thoughts of peace and not of evil,
to give you a future and a hope.

JEREMIAH 29:11

Prayer Notes

What Can Keep Us from Fearing the Future?

Lord, I want to be able to say, "I have fought the good fight, I have finished the race, I have kept the faith" (2 Timothy 4:7). Thank You that "You will show me the path of life; in Your presence is fullness of joy; at Your right hand are pleasures forevermore" (Psalm 16:11). Thank You that because I have put my faith in You, I have Your Holy Spirit within me, and this seals my future. Help me to keep my eyes on You and not the predictors of disaster who don't know You. They don't determine my future—You do. Help me to forget "those things which are behind" and reach "forward to those things which are ahead" (Philippians 3:13).

In Jesus' name I pray.

Mark the blameless man,
and observe the upright;
for the future of that man is peace.

PSALM 37:37

Prayer Notes

_____

_____

_____

_____

_____

_____

_____

_____

_____

_____

_____

What Can Keep Us from Fearing the Future?

Lord, I don't want to worry about the future because I know my future is in Your hands. I don't want to judge my future by my past because Your mercies "are new every morning" (Lamentations 3:23). Help me not to feel sorry for myself when things don't go according to my plans. Instead, give me faith to believe that because I have committed my life to You, my life is proceeding according to *Your* plan. Help me to grow in faith, trusting that Your plans for my life are good. You have said many times in Your Word, "Do not be afraid," "Do not worry," "Do not be anxious." Enable me to have strong faith to believe that at all times.

In Jesus' name I pray.

*Do not worry about your life, what you will eat
or what you will drink; nor about your body,
what you will put on.
Is not life more than food and
the body more than clothing?*

MATTHEW 6:25

Prayer Notes

_____

_____

_____

_____

_____

_____

_____

_____

_____

_____

What Can Keep Us from Fearing the Future?

Lord, thank You that I don't have to live in fear of the future. Your Word says that those who believe in You will never be shaken, and we don't have to live in fear of bad news. Thank You that You are with me, giving me peace, guidance, and joy even in the midst of difficult times. I know my future is determined by the steps I take today. Help me to walk with You every day and to consider my future with every decision I make. Help me to remember to not make plans without consulting You and waiting on You for Your leading and guidance. Give me peace about my future because it is found in You.

In Jesus' name I pray.

Surely he will never be shaken;
the righteous will be in everlasting remembrance.
He will not be afraid of evil tidings;
*his heart is steadfast, trusting in the L*ORD.

PSALM 112:6-7

Prayer Notes

_____

_____

_____

_____

_____

_____

_____

_____

_____

_____

What Can Keep Us from Fearing the Future?

Lord, help me to live with a sense of Your purpose for my life. No matter what happens—even when I have to go through times of grief or suffering—I pray I will think of those times as not worthy to be compared to the future glory of being with You. Help me to wait peacefully and calmly on You and not listen to godless people telling me what my future will be. They don't determine my future—*You* do. You are the God of new beginnings, and I pray You will give me a renewed sense of purpose, a new commitment to prayer, and a fresh dedication to serving You. Help me to shut off the world and listen to Your voice and Word speaking to my heart.

In Jesus' name I pray.

I consider that the sufferings of this present time are not worthy to be compared with the glory which shall be revealed in us.

ROMANS 8:18

Prayer Notes

_____

_____

_____

_____

_____

_____

_____

_____

_____

_____

_____

What Can Keep Us from Fearing the Future?

Lord, I love Your promises to those who wait on You—that my strength will be renewed and that I can run and not be weary. Especially in times when I am worn out by the things I see that frighten me, help me to "lay aside every weight, and the sin which so easily ensnares" me and help me to "run with endurance the race that is set" before me (Hebrews 12:1).

I pray You will raise up an army of prayer warriors all over the world who will pray every day that all the enemy is planning will not come to pass, and that Your plans to protect Your righteous believers will prevail. We pray that good and godly people will come to power in every country, city, town, and community.

In Jesus' name I pray.

Those who wait on the LORD
shall renew their strength;
they shall mount up with wings like eagles,
they shall run and not be weary,
they shall walk and not faint.

ISAIAH 40:31

Prayer Notes

Other Books by Stormie Omartian

OUT OF DARKNESS

In this poignant true story, there is help and hope for anyone who has been scarred by the past or feels imprisoned by deep emotional needs. Stormie shares from her own life how God can bring life out of death and light out of darkness.

LEAD ME, HOLY SPIRIT

The Holy Spirit wants those who know Him to hear when He speaks to their heart, soul, and spirit. He wants to help believers enter into the relationship with God they yearn for, the wholeness and freedom God has for them, and the place of safety they can only find by following His leading to the center of His perfect will.

PRAYER WARRIOR

For every Christian who wants a meaningful prayer life that is more than just asking for blessings, bestselling author Stormie Omartian shows you how to pray with strength and purpose—prayers resulting in great victory, not only personally but also in advancing God's kingdom and glory.

JUST ENOUGH LIGHT FOR THE STEP I'M ON

Anyone going through changes or difficult times will appreciate Stormie's honesty, candor, and advice based on the Word of God and her experiences in this book that is perfect for the pressures of today's world.